BREAKING THROUGH SHADOWS:

A Comprehensive Guide to Overcoming Depression

Dr. Morgan E. Maxwells

TABLE OF CONTENT

INTRODUCTION

Depression affects millions of individuals worldwide, casting a dismal shadow over their lives. It is a complicated and devastating mental health disease that may leave persons feeling confined and isolated. However, there is hope. This book, "Breaking Through Shadows," attempts to give a detailed and sympathetic explanation of depression, giving practical ideas and resources for discovering the route to recovery and recovering a happy life. By addressing the reasons, symptoms, and numerous treatment choices, this book will lead you toward a better future.

CHAPTER 1: Understanding Depression

Section 1: Defining Depression and its ts Influence on Persons

Depression is a mental health illness characterized by persistent feelings of melancholy, despair, and a lack of interest in things that were formerly pleasant. It goes beyond regular emotions of sorrow or brief mood changes and profoundly disrupts a person's daily functioning, relationships, and general well-being. Depression may afflict individuals of various ages, genders, and backgrounds.

The effect of depression on people may be severe. It impacts not just their mental condition but also their physical health, cognitive ability, and social connections. Some frequent impacts of depression include:

Emotional Impact:
Intense emotions of melancholy, emptiness, and despair. Individuals may suffer a loss of pleasure or interest in things they formerly loved, resulting in a sense of emotional numbness.

Physical Impact:
Depression frequently shows physical, producing symptoms such as exhaustion, changes in food and weight, sleep abnormalities (insomnia or excessive sleeping), and unexplained physical pain or discomfort.

Cognitive Impact:
Depression may affect focus, memory, and decision-making ability. Individuals may feel problems concentrating, have trouble making judgments, or display a major decline in productivity.

Social Impact:
Depression may strain relationships, as people may withdraw from social contacts, feel socially alienated, or have difficulties sustaining intimate friendships. It might also influence job or school performance and limit participation in everyday activities.

Section 2: The varied kinds of depression

Depression may show in numerous ways, each with its distinct features and durations. Some typical kinds of depression include:

•Major Depressive Disorder (MDD):
This is the most frequent kind of depression. It entails having chronic emotions of melancholy, lack of interest or pleasure, changes in eating or weight, sleep issues, poor energy, feelings of worthlessness or guilt, trouble focusing, and occasionally reoccurring thoughts of death or suicide. MDD normally lasts for at least two weeks.

•Persistent Depressive Disorder (PDD):
Also known as dysthymia, PDD requires suffering a persistent low mood for a minimum of two years. While the symptoms may be less severe than MDD, they are more persistent.

•Seasonal Affective Disorder (SAD):
SAD is a kind of depression that follows a seasonal rhythm, generally appearing during the winter months when there is less sunshine. Symptoms include poor mood, increased sleep, weight gain, and reduced energy.

•Postpartum Depression:
This kind of depression affects women after giving delivery. It encompasses emotions of severe grief, worry, and weariness that might interfere with a mother's ability to care for herself and her infant. It is vital to get quick medical assistance for postpartum depression. Bipolar condition: While not entirely a depressive condition, bipolar disorder comprises alternating bouts of depression and mania (elevated mood). The depressed episodes of bipolar disorder are comparable to MDD but are followed by moments of increased energy, racing thoughts, and impulsivity.

Section 3: Recognizing common symptoms and warning signs

Recognizing the symptoms and warning signs of depression is vital for early intervention and getting appropriate support. Common symptoms include:

•Persistent emotions of melancholy, emptiness, or despair.
•Loss of interest or pleasure in activities formerly liked.
•Changes in appetite and weight (significant weight loss or increase).
•Sleep disorders (insomnia or excessive sleeping).
•Fatigue or lack of energy.
•Difficulty focusing, making judgments, or remembering things.
•Feelings of worthlessness, excessive guilt, or self-blame.
•Restlessness or delayed motions.
•Recurring thoughts of death or suicide.

It is crucial to remember that not everyone will have all these symptoms, and the intensity may vary.

CHAPTER 2: Unveiling the Causes

Understanding the origins of mental health difficulties is vital to design successful treatment programs and support measures. Mental diseases may emerge from a mix of numerous variables, including biological, environmental, psychological, and social factors. Let's investigate each of these aspects in detail:

•Biological factors:
Biological factors contribute to mental health difficulties via genetic predispositions, brain chemistry abnormalities, and hormone disruptions. Genetics have a part in defining an individual's vulnerability to various mental diseases. For example, illnesses like schizophrenia and bipolar disorder have been proven to have a hereditary component. Brain chemistry abnormalities, such as aberrant amounts of neurotransmitters like serotonin or dopamine, may impair mood, behavior, and general mental well-being.

Additionally, hormonal abnormalities, such as those observed in illnesses like thyroid problems or hormonal shifts during puberty or menopause, may impair mental health.

•*Environmental factors:*

Environmental factors cover many environmental variables that might lead to mental health disorders. Life events, such as the death of a loved one, divorce, job loss, or financial troubles, may cause or aggravate mental health issues like melancholy or anxiety. Traumatic situations, such as physical or sexual abuse, violence, or accidents, may have long-lasting consequences on mental well-being. Chronic stress, stemming from continuing problems, job pressure, or marital issues, may also significantly damage mental health.

Additionally, factors including exposure to pollutants, poor diet, and drug misuse may lead to mental health disorders.

•*Psychological factors:*

Psychological variables relate to an individual's ideas, emotions, and cognitive processes. Negative thought patterns and cognitive distortions may play a key influence in the development and maintenance of mental health issues. For example, persons with depression typically have negative ideas about themselves, their future, and the world, leading to a cycle of low mood and despair. Cognitive distortions include skewed or illogical thought processes, such as black-and-white thinking, overgeneralization, or catastrophizing, which may lead to anxiety and other mental health issues.

•*Social factors:*
Social factors relate to the social environment and interpersonal connections that impact mental health. Social isolation, a lack of supporting connections, or a restricted social network might raise the risk of mental health disorders. Human beings are social animals, and a feeling of belonging and social support is crucial for general well-being.

Additionally, cultural expectations, such as unattainable standards of beauty, success, or conformity, may contribute to stress, poor self-esteem, and mental health difficulties. Discrimination, stigma, and marginalization based on variables like race, gender, sexuality, or disability may also influence mental well-being. It's crucial to emphasize that mental health concerns are complicated and multidimensional, and individual experiences may contain a mix of these elements.

The relationship between these elements might be complicated and unique to each individual. Identifying and understanding the underlying causes of mental health difficulties may aid in developing appropriate treatments, treatment regimens, and support networks to match the particular needs of people. A comprehensive approach that takes into consideration biological, environmental, psychological, and social aspects is frequently important for fostering mental well-being and healing.

CHAPTER 3: Seeking Professional Help

In this chapter, we will discuss the necessity of receiving professional care for mental health difficulties. We will address the importance of professional diagnosis and assessment, present an overview of mental health specialists, look into various forms of therapy, and analyze the function of drugs in treatment.

The necessity of professional diagnosis and assessment:

When it comes to mental health, receiving a professional diagnosis and evaluation is vital. Mental health professionals have the competence and knowledge to detect and diagnose mental diseases properly. They employ established diagnostic criteria, such as the Diagnostic and Statistical Manual of Mental Disorders (DSM-5), to identify and categorize mental health disorders. A correct diagnosis assists in identifying the underlying causes of the symptoms and leads to the formulation of a suitable treatment strategy.

Overview of mental health professionals:

There are numerous sorts of mental health experts that specialize in diagnosing and treating mental health disorders. Here are three basic types:

•***Psychiatrists:*** Psychiatrists are medical professionals who specialize in mental health. They can diagnose mental problems, administer medicine, and give a holistic approach to therapy. They may also give counseling in combination with drug management.

•***Psychologists:*** Psychologists have a Ph.D. degree in psychology and are skilled in assessing and diagnosing mental health disorders. They typically offer therapy and counseling services utilizing evidence-based methodologies. However, they cannot prescribe drugs.

•***Therapists/Counselors:*** Therapists or counselors might have diverse backgrounds and certifications, such as certified professional counselors (LPC), licensed clinical social workers (LCSW), or marriage and family therapists (MFT). They give therapy and counseling services to individuals, couples, or families to treat different mental health difficulties.

Different methods of therapy:
Therapy is a vital component of mental health therapy. Here are a few regularly utilized therapy approaches:

•**Cognitive-Behavioral Therapy (CBT):** CBT focuses on recognizing and altering negative thought patterns and behaviors that lead to mental health difficulties. It seeks to modify problematic beliefs and actions and replace them with more adaptive ones.

•**Interpersonal Therapy (IPT):** IPT focuses on enhancing interpersonal interactions and treating particular difficulties in partnerships. It helps people recognize and manage conflicts, communication challenges, and social obstacles that may contribute to their mental health concerns.

•**Additional forms of treatment**: There are several additional therapeutic techniques, such as psychodynamic therapy, dialectical behavior therapy (DBT), mindfulness-based therapy, and family therapy. Each method has its distinct ideas and tactics, and the choice of treatment relies on the individual's requirements and preferences.

•**Medication choices and their function in treatment:** Medication may be a vital aspect of mental health therapy, particularly for specific problems including depression, anxiety disorders, bipolar disorder, and schizophrenia. Psychiatrists are authorized to prescribe medicine depending on the individual's diagnosis and symptoms. Medication may help ease symptoms, calm mood, and enhance general performance. However, it is crucial to remember that medicine alone may not be adequate for full treatment, and therapy typically complements medication for maximum outcomes.

In summary, obtaining professional treatment is vital for resolving mental health difficulties. Mental health specialists, such as psychiatrists, psychologists, and therapists, play key roles in diagnosis, counseling, and medication administration. Different forms of treatment, such as CBT and IPT, provide helpful techniques to address diverse mental health difficulties. Medication, provided by psychiatrists, may be effective in combination with treatment. Remember, treatment regimens are customized to individual requirements, and it's necessary to talk with a specialist to decide the most suitable course of action.

CHAPTER 4: Self-Help Strategies

Self-help methods are skills and activities that people may apply to increase their mental health and well-being. These practices allow people to take an active part in their self-care and may be effective in reducing stress, increasing mood, and strengthening overall psychological resilience. Let's investigate some typical self-help practices in detail:

•***Developing a support network:*** Building and cultivating a support network is vital for sustaining healthy mental health. This network might include friends, family members, or support groups of folks who have similar experiences. Having a support system gives emotional support, a feeling of belonging, and an avenue for communicating worries and issues. Engaging with helpful folks may give encouragement, affirmation, and practical counsel during stressful times.

•**Self-care techniques:** Engaging in self-care activities is crucial for sustaining mental well-being. This involves taking care of physical health since the mind and body are intertwined. Regular exercise produces endorphins, which boost happy sensations and decrease stress.

Eating a balanced diet with sufficient nutrition may give the body and brain vital nutrients for optimum functioning. Adequate sleep is also vital for mental health, as it helps the body and mind to relax and renew.

Cognitive restructuring: Cognitive restructuring entails confronting and transforming unfavorable ideas and beliefs that lead to suffering or unpleasant emotions. By being aware of negative thinking patterns and cognitive distortions (e.g., catastrophizing, overgeneralization), people may learn to replace them with more realistic and optimistic views. This procedure aids in lowering anxiety, sadness, and other mental health issues. Cognitive restructuring frequently entails reviewing data, challenging assumptions, and reframing thinking in a more balanced and adaptable way.

•**Relaxation methods:** Relaxation techniques are beneficial in lowering stress, fostering tranquility, and enhancing general mental well-being. Some regularly utilized relaxation methods include:

~*Mindfulness:* Mindfulness entails paying attention to the current moment without judgment. It helps people grow mindfulness, improve self-compassion, and lessen rumination or anxieties about the past or future.

~Meditation: Meditation methods, such as focused attention or loving-kindness meditation, induce relaxation, increase concentration, and boost emotional well-being. Regular meditation may decrease stress and build resilience.

~*Deep breathing exercises:* Deep breathing exercises entail slow, deep breaths, focused on inhaling and exhaling.

This approach increases the body's relaxation response, decreases heart rate, and reduces anxiety and stress. Incorporating these self-help practices into everyday routines may have a good influence on mental health. It's crucial to remember that self-help tactics complement professional aid but may not be adequate for severe or chronic mental health disorders. If people are suffering substantial distress, it is vital to seek help from mental health specialists who can give personalized treatments and support.

Additionally, self-help tactics are very personalized, and it may take time to identify the mix of strategies that work best for each person. Experimenting with numerous tactics and approaches may help people find what resonates with them and supports their specific needs and preferences. Regular practice and consistency are crucial to getting long-term advantages from these self-help tactics.

CHAPTER 5: Lifestyle Changes for Recovery

When working towards mental health recovery, lifestyle adjustments have a vital role in improving general well-being. Making good alterations to everyday routines and behaviors may lead to greater mood, less stress, and enhanced resilience. Let's go into the specifics of several crucial lifestyle modifications for recovery:

•***Creating a balanced routine and establishing realistic goals:*** Establishing a balanced daily routine may give stability and structure, which is especially beneficial for persons coping with mental health difficulties. A routine helps manage sleep cycles, eating habits, and daily activities, giving a feeling of control and predictability. It's necessary to develop realistic and attainable objectives that fit with individual talents and circumstances. Break down major chores into smaller, achievable stages to prevent feeling overwhelmed. Celebrating little victories may enhance motivation and create a feeling of accomplishment.

•*Exploring the advantages of physical exercise and its influence on mood:*
Engaging in regular physical exercise has several advantages for mental health. Exercise causes the production of endorphins, chemicals that boost emotions of pleasure and decrease stress. Regular physical exercise may decrease symptoms of sadness and anxiety, improve mood, raise energy levels, and enhance general cognitive performance. Activities like walking, running, yoga, dancing, or any sort of exercise that one loves might be helpful. Incorporating physical exercise into one's regimen may be an empowering and good step toward rehabilitation.

•*The significance of a good diet and its link to mental well-being:* A balanced and nutritious diet is vital for both physical and mental health. Certain nutrients have a significant role in brain function and mental well-being. Diets rich in fruits, vegetables, whole grains, lean meats, and healthy fats may promote good brain function. Omega-3 fatty acids, present in fatty fish, flaxseeds, and walnuts, have been connected with enhanced mood and decreased risk of depression. On the other side, excessive intake of processed meals, sugary snacks, and stimulants like coffee may adversely affect mood and worsen feelings of anxiety.

•*Managing stress and adopting stress-reducing activities:*
Stress is a normal part of life, but prolonged or severe stress may have harmful consequences on mental

health. Managing stress is key to healing. Mindfulness activities, such as meditation and deep breathing exercises, may help people become more aware of their stresses and create healthy reactions to them. Engaging in hobbies, artistic interests, or spending time in nature may be helpful stress-reducing activities. Learning time management and prioritizing skills may also help lessen feelings of overload and improve overall stress management.

It's crucial to note that lifestyle modifications for recovery are not one-size-fits-all, and people may need to experiment to discover what works best for them. Additionally, rehabilitation is a slow process, and setbacks are a normal part of the trip. Being patient and sympathetic with oneself is vital during this period.

While lifestyle modifications may be helpful for many people, they may not be adequate for severe or chronic mental health disorders. Professional help from mental health specialists, such as therapists, counselors, or psychiatrists, may complement lifestyle modifications and give targeted treatments and direction. An integrated strategy that incorporates self-help tactics, lifestyle adjustments, and professional support may offer a complete foundation for mental health rehabilitation.

CHAPTER 6: Building Resilience

Resilience refers to the capacity to adapt, bounce back, and prosper in the face of adversity or tough conditions. It is a critical talent for sustaining mental well-being and navigating through life's ups and downs. Building resilience entails adopting a set of attitudes, abilities, and practices that may help people manage stress, overcome challenges, and retain a positive perspective. Let's analyze in depth some crucial factors of creating resilience:

•Developing self-compassion and self-acceptance: Self-compassion means treating oneself with kindness, understanding, and acceptance, particularly during tough circumstances. It is about realizing that everyone faces failures and problems, and it's alright to be flawed. Practicing self-compassion entails being attentive to one's own needs, embracing self-care, and being kind to oneself while confronting problems. This approach helps people create a robust and supportive connection with themselves.

•Enhancing emotional intelligence and developing coping skills: Emotional intelligence refers to the capacity to detect, comprehend, and control one's emotions successfully. It entails growing self-awareness, empathy towards others, and healthy methods of expressing and controlling emotions. By developing emotional intelligence, people may better handle difficult circumstances, communicate effectively, and adjust to changes. Developing coping skills, such as problem-solving, stress management strategies, and positive reframing, empowers people with the ability to handle problems and healthily control emotions.

•Nurturing healthy connections and creating a support system: healthy relationships and a robust support system are crucial for resilience. Nurturing good ties with family, friends, or support groups gives emotional support, validation, and encouragement through stressful times. Good connections may bring a feeling of belonging, trust, and teamwork. Being able to seek aid and depend on others for support may considerably boost resilience.

•Finding meaning and purpose in life: Having a sense of meaning and purpose in life adds to resilience and general well-being. It entails defining personal beliefs, interests, and objectives that give life purpose. Engaging in activities or pursuing objectives that correspond with one's beliefs and interests may bring a feeling of contentment and drive, especially in the face of hardship. Connecting with a sense of purpose may help people develop resilience and face problems with more drive.

Building resilience is a constant process that takes experience and purposeful effort. It is crucial to remember that resilience does not entail ignoring or concealing unpleasant feelings. Rather, it entails noticing and processing emotions while having a happy and flexible mentality. Seeking help from mental health specialists, such as therapists or counselors, may give direction and tools for strengthening resilience.

It's crucial to remember that developing resilience is very personal, and various tactics may connect with different individuals. Exploring multiple strategies and ideas might help people determine what works best for them. With time and experience, increasing resilience may promote mental well-being and give people the ability to negotiate life's obstacles more effectively.

CHAPTER 7: Preventing Relapse

When people are on the road to recovery from mental health difficulties, avoiding relapse is a critical element of preserving long-term well-being. Relapse refers to a return or worsening of symptoms following a period of recovery. To avoid relapse, people may use techniques that entail detecting warning signals, establishing a relapse prevention plan, practicing continual self-care and stress management, and keeping open communication with their support network. Let's investigate each of these features in detail:

Recognizing the indications of probable relapse:
Being aware of the warning signals and early indicators of relapse is vital for adopting preventative actions. These indicators might vary from person to person but may include changes in mood, sleep habits, food, energy levels, or a sensation of rising stress or overload. People must get acquainted with their unique warning signals and pay attention to any alterations or trends that might suggest a possible relapse. This self-awareness enables prompt intervention.

Developing a relapse prevention plan:

Creating a relapse prevention strategy entails describing methods and activities that may help people manage and decrease the risk of recurrence. The plan may contain particular coping skills, such as participating in frequent therapy sessions, joining support groups, practicing self-care activities, or applying specialized approaches like cognitive-behavioral therapy (CBT) tools. The plan should also identify possible triggers and stressors and explain ways for managing and dealing with them effectively.

Practicing continuing self-care and stress management: Continuing to prioritize self-care and stress management is vital for avoiding relapse. Self-care techniques may involve maintaining a healthy lifestyle, such as participating in regular exercise, eating a balanced diet, getting adequate sleep, and engaging in hobbies that offer pleasure and relaxation. Managing stress is also crucial, and people may adopt stress-reducing practices such as mindfulness, meditation, deep breathing exercises, or participating in hobbies or activities that offer stress reduction. It is crucial to proactively manage stress and take frequent breaks to prevent being overwhelmed.

Maintaining an open channel of contact with your support network: Having a strong support network and having open contact with them is vital in avoiding relapse. Regularly engaging with friends, family members, or support groups may give emotional support, understanding, and encouragement. Sharing worries, struggles, and triumphs with trustworthy others may help individuals gain perspective, get affirmation, and obtain further resources or direction if required. Being honest and upfront about one's experiences and needs is vital in obtaining continued help.

Consistency and dedication to these preventative techniques are crucial in avoiding relapse. It is vital to remember that relapse does not represent failure but rather a chance for learning and progress. If relapse does occur, it is crucial to seek out mental health specialists for advice and support.

Preventing relapse is a continual process, and measures may need to be altered or updated over time. Each person's relapse prevention strategy will be unique to their circumstances and requirements. Regularly reassessing and modifying the relapse prevention strategy helps guarantee its efficacy in promoting long-term recovery and well-being.

CHAPTER 8: Supporting Others with Depression

When someone we care about is suffering from depression, giving support and understanding may make a major difference in their road toward recovery. It is crucial to handle the problem with understanding, tolerance, and a desire to learn. Supporting those with depression entails knowing how to assist, effective communication, supporting professional help-seeking, and offering continuing support. Let's investigate each of these features in detail:

•**Understanding how to aid a loved one with depression:** Educating yourself on depression is vital for understanding the disorder and its effect on people. Learn about the symptoms, causes, and various treatment options. This understanding can help you tackle the problem with sensitivity and remove any misconceptions or stigma around mental health. Understanding that depression is a genuine and legitimate disorder may establish a supportive atmosphere for your loved one.

•**Effective communication and active listening:** Open and non-judgmental communication is crucial when assisting someone with depression. Encourage your loved one to communicate their emotions and opinions honestly. Practice active listening by giving them your complete attention, keeping eye contact, and responding with empathy and understanding. Avoid belittling their experiences or providing fast remedies. Instead, recognize their sentiments, affirm their experiences, and let them know you are there to support them.

•Encouraging professional help-seeking: Depression is a complicated mental health problem that typically needs professional attention. Encourage your loved one to get treatment from mental health specialists, such as therapists, counselors, or psychiatrists. Offer aid in identifying acceptable resources, such as suggesting trustworthy specialists or offering information about therapeutic alternatives and support groups. Let them know that obtaining expert treatment is a great step towards recovery and that they don't have to face it alone.

•Providing continual support and encouragement: Supporting someone with depression entails being there for them regularly. Offer your support, but also respect their limits and speed. Let them know you are willing to listen, spend time together, or participate in things they like. Small gestures of kindness, such as checking in periodically, sending encouraging notes, or volunteering to accompany them to appointments, may have a tremendous difference. Encourage them to participate in

self-care activities, maintain a healthy lifestyle, and remind them of their strengths and progress.
It is vital to remember that assisting someone with depression may be emotionally exhausting. Take care of your well-being and seek help from your network or specialists if required. Additionally, if you observe any symptoms of self-harm, or suicidal thoughts, or the individual is in imminent danger, it is vital to engage emergency authorities or a mental health crisis hotline for urgent help.

Each person's experience with depression is unique, so modify your approach to the individual's requirements. Patience, empathy, and continued support may play a vital part in supporting your loved one on their road to recovery.

CONCLUSION

Depression is a hard and complicated mental health illness, but it is vital to remember that recovery is attainable. Throughout this book, "Breaking Through Shadows," we have studied different elements of depression, including its causes, seeking professional assistance, self-help tactics, lifestyle changes, building resilience, preventing recurrence, and supporting others. By receiving an understanding of depression and employing the skills and tactics offered, people may engage on a transforming path towards recovery and a better future.

Understanding the causes of depression, including biological, environmental, psychological, and social components, helps people appreciate the complexity of the disorder. Seeking expert aid and having a thorough diagnosis are vital for optimal therapy and support. Mental health specialists, such as psychiatrists, psychologists, and therapists, provide several therapy and pharmaceutical alternatives that may greatly benefit the healing process.

In addition to professional aid, applying self-help measures is vital. Developing a social network, practicing self-care, confronting negative thinking patterns, and implementing relaxation methods are all crucial stages in treating depression. Making lifestyle adjustments, such as developing a balanced routine, participating in physical exercise, keeping a good diet, and managing stress, may assist in overall well-being and healing.

Building resilience is another crucial part of conquering depression. Cultivating self-compassion, boosting emotional intelligence, maintaining healthy relationships, and finding meaning and purpose in life all contribute to creating resilience and the capacity to adapt and flourish in the face of adversity.

Preventing relapse is a major concern in sustaining long-term mental well-being. Recognizing warning signals, adopting a relapse prevention plan, practicing continual self-care and stress management, and keeping open communication with a support network are important tactics for avoiding relapse and remaining on the road to recovery.

Finally, helping those with depression needs understanding, good communication, promoting professional help-seeking, and offering continual support and encouragement. By fostering a supportive and caring atmosphere, you may have a beneficial influence on your loved one's road to recovery.

Remember, conquering depression requires time, tolerance, and dedication to self-care. It is crucial to call out for assistance, whether it's from mental health specialists, support groups, or loved ones. With the correct information, skills, and support, it is possible to break free from the hold of sadness and construct a satisfying and meaningful life. Even in the darkest of circumstances, there is always hope.